How to Write Nonfiction eBooks

A Proven 17-Step Plan for Beginners

By

Henri Junttila

How to Write Nonfiction eBooks

Table of Contents

Introduction

When I wrote my first book, I was swallowed by fear. I was paralyzed at the mere thought of writing a book.

I've since realized that I make it harder than it has to be. Luckily, I've learned to follow my inspiration. I'm afraid—like anyone else—but I follow my inner nudges, and it is those inner nudges that have led me to write these very words.

You see, this isn't a book about getting rich with Kindle (or ebooks). This isn't about cranking out one book per week of questionable quality.

This book is about writing nonfiction ebooks, specifically how-to books. Most of the books I write are shorter, around 12,000-20,000 words, because I want to tackle one topic instead of trying to cover everything.

This book is about my writing process, which I've honed through years of practice. I've made a living online since 2009, and today I spend my days enjoying life, my relationships, and my children (I became a father in late 2011).

My writing process allows me to have fun while I write. I'm able to write books fast without skimping on quality.

I use my whole being when I write, meaning my conscious and subconscious minds. This may sound mystical, but it's not. In this book, you will discover a step-by-step process for writing a nonfiction book, even if you've never written a book before.

My goal with my books—and with anything I produce—is to help my reader, customer, or client. I'm not here to fool you, because I've been fooled myself.

I've wasted over $10,000+ on learning how to make a living online, but that's another story.

On top of that, I'm a perfectionist. I'm afraid. I'm not the world's best writer. Yet I write, because I love to write.

My guess is that you like writing as well, and that you want to write a book. If that's the case, you're in the right place. There will be no huffing and puffing here, just helpful, practical, and simple tips that will help you translate your inspiration into words.

How to Read This Book

This book is written in a logical, step-by-step fashion. The best way to read it is to read it through once and then use it as a reference guide as you write your book.

If that doesn't fit your style, feel free to jump around as much as you wish. Each chapter can be read independently as I share the what, why, and how of that topic as well as examples of what I did and the mistakes I made. I end each chapter with action steps to help you move forward.

In short, each chapter is logically structured, and each chapter takes you through my book writing process in a logical, easy-to-understand manner.

When you're ready, turn the page, and let's jump right in.

Free Gift

Before you jump into the content, I wanted to mention that at the end of this book, you will find a bonus workbook that contains all of the questions and action steps.

I've put this together so you don't have to go digging through the book every time you need to reference something. Plus, the workbook will keep you on track as you write your own book.

Now let's jump into the first chapter.

1. The Intersection

The absolute first question you have to ask yourself is: What do I feel inspired to write about?

When your writing comes from your heart, it touches people.

Now, you could stop reading right here and write the book you feel inspired to write. But if you're like most people, you may need help in tapping into the language of your audience, which allows you to reach more people and sell more books.

That's why this first chapter is about finding the intersection. Few books talk about the intersection. They talk about finding profitable topics, but they forget other crucial parts. Because this is not just about making money, but about contributing to the world in a meaningful way.

The problem is that there is no formula for writing books. You have to write, put books out there, and see what sticks. Most people want guarantees. The guarantee isn't found in a perfect idea or book. It's found in experimentation, in writing more books and noticing what works.

What is the Intersection?

I talk about the intersection when I help people build businesses around their passion, and it applies to writing books as well.

What is the intersection? The intersection is:

- What you want to do

- What you know (or have a story around)
- What people are interested in

This doesn't have to be a complicated process, but finding some sort of an intersection for the book you want to write will help you get more readers and sales.

When you're first getting started, you may not know what your intersection is. That's fine, and to be expected. All that is required is that you do your best and keep writing.

Reasons to Use the Intersection

The biggest reason is that your book has a higher chance of success. When you give people what they want, they'll be more likely to purchase your book.

You will also be motivated to write more books, because you will follow your inspiration while selling books and having an impact. You won't write just for money. You will tap into your inner urge, which holds energy and power.

When you do your research, you also uncover what language your audience uses. By language, I mean what words they use to search for books and information, and what kind of book titles they respond to.

Now let's dive into how to actually find the intersection.

How to Find the Intersection

The intersection may seem complex at first, but in reality, there are only three parts to it, and you can ignore parts that you don't resonate with.

Here are the three parts of the intersection:

1. What Do You Feel Inspired to Write?

In order for you to be inspired, there has to be someone doing the inspiring. Your inspiration comes from a deeper part of you. You could call it God, the Universe, higher self, heart, or simply the subconscious mind. It doesn't matter what you call it.

What matters is that you follow your inspiration. I've found that when I follow my inspiration, while taking into account the other parts of the intersection, I have more fun while writing my book, and my books are better received.

You might ask: How do I discover what I'm inspired to write about?

That's a tough question, because there is no pat answer. When I get inspired, I feel pulled towards a topic. For example, when I had the idea to write this book, I had already received questions from my readers. They wanted to know more. I also felt positive about writing the book. I felt inspired and ideas flowed to me. That's how I knew I was inspired to write this.

A good place to start is to look around you. Look at the clothes you wear, the books you read, the websites you visit, and what you find yourself drawn to. When you do this, you notice patterns and themes.

But if you're like most people, you may have no idea. Don't worry. Don't take it too seriously. Write the book you can write, because it is through action that clarity comes.

2. What Do You Know?

Your story is powerful. Readers need to hear your story in order to trust you. Our brains are hardwired to listen to stories.

When you know a topic well, you can write from your heart. For example, all the books I've written are books on topics I know well. I felt inspired to write them, and I knew the topic, so writing them was fairly easy. I say fairly, because I did struggle, like any other writer.

When I write a book just to make money, and ignore my heart, it usually ends up in failure. I don't know why, but there's no energy in it. Some people may be able to go after money, but I know that it doesn't lead to happiness, not for me.

3. What Do People Want?

The last, and perhaps the most important, part is to look at what people want. What frustrations, problems, and fears do readers have? How can you help them?

The best way to do this is to look at what people are buying on Amazon. Pay close attention to the paid sales rank, which you will find in the product details section under each book. Look for books that have around #20,000 paid sales rank, which means they're selling around 4-6 copies per day.

Don't just settle for one book, but look for several books that are selling at least moderately well. You're looking for proof that the book you want to write is already selling. I'm not suggesting you plagiarize. I'm suggesting you look at what topics are selling and put your unique spin on it.

Amazon is a great place to start your research. Look at what's already selling and start there.

The truth is that you may not stand out with your first book. It may not sell well, and that's okay, because you will keep writing. This isn't about writing an amazing first book. This is about putting in the work and allowing yourself to get good at the craft.

To increase your chances of standing out, focus your book on a specific topic. So not just "Organic Growing," but something like "How to Grow Organic Tomatoes Indoors."

A Real World Example

Let's look at a real example from one of my books. The book in question is *Write Blog Posts Readers Love: A Step-By-Step Guide.*

It all started with inspiration. I had just finished writing *Follow Your Heart: 21 Days to a Happier, More Fulfilling Life*, and I felt exhausted. I didn't think I would be writing another book anytime soon, but the very next day I felt inspired to start writing.

Writing blog posts is a topic I'm very knowledgeable about, because I've built up a 10,000+ subscriber blog and I've been making a living with my writing since 2009.

The topic of writing blog posts popped up because:

- A few of my popular posts were on writing blog posts and articles
- I'd often get questions about blogging and writing
- I had an online course that was doing well on the subject
- I felt inspired to write about blogging

So the next step was to go to Amazon and look at how blogging books were doing.

I found two or three books. They weren't selling well at the time. I think their paid sales rank was around #30,000-40,000, which equates to about 2-4 copies per day. But I was okay with that. I knew I'd be writing more books, so any one book wasn't going to make or break me.

So this may be an example of what not to do, because my book hasn't been selling extremely well (1-2 copies per day at most). But I decided to write what I felt like writing.

After I'd done my preliminary research, I looked at what problems people had when writing blog posts. I went back to my own data and notes, but I also looked at Amazon reviews.

As you can see, my research process is quite simple. This is what works for me, and it's up to you to find what works for you.

A Bonus Tip

If you want to discover what to put in your book, you can take a look at the table of contents of popular books in the topic you want to write about.

Another way is to look at reviews. Look at the good and bad reviews, and you will discover what people love and hate about the book. Keep your notepad handy so you can write down relevant information.

Be careful with this though because you can get discouraged while reading negative reviews.

A Mistake to Avoid

The biggest mistake I want you to avoid at this stage is perfectionism. What stops most people from writing the book they want to write is thinking that they aren't ready for it or that circumstances aren't right.

The stars may not be aligned, but they don't have to be. You just have to start, because once you start, you learn, and you improve. So even if your first books end up a disaster, you have to write them in order to become the writer you were meant to be.

Action Steps

In each chapter, I'll include action steps that summarize what you've learned. This will help you understand and apply what you've read. The action steps for this chapter are:

1. Inspiration. What do you feel inspired to write? It doesn't have to be the book you've fantasizing about for the last decade. I recommend you start small. It's less scary and you will have more fun.

2. Story. What do you know, or where do you have a story to tell? What problems have you overcome? When you know a topic, it shows, and people enjoy hearing your perspective. You don't have to be an all-knowing expert. You just have to know more than your readers, and you have to have a story to tell.

3. Demand. What do people want? Take a look on Amazon and find what's popular. Look for several books in your topic area that have a #20,000 sales rank or lower. Use that to prune your list of book ideas. If you don't know what to write about, then pick something and get started. When you take action, you get clarity.

Now let's move on to coming up with a title for your book.

2. The Title

Once you've found the intersection for your book, you're ready to proceed to coming up with your book title, or the name for your book.

And remember, the title doesn't have to be perfect. In fact, let it be messy, because if you're anything like me, you have a tendency to try to find the perfect title, and the perfect topic.

It probably won't happen. Believe me. I've tried. The key then is to write, and write some more. Do your best and get started.

What is a Title?

A title tells your reader that he or she will receive value from reading your book. A good title grabs attention and increases the desirability of your book.

The bolder your promise, the more attention you will get. But be careful of making a promise that sounds unbelievable.

In short, your book title is nothing more than a promise of what's to come if people buy your book.

Why Your Title is Essential

Your title draws people in. Cosmopolitan Magazine sells because their curiosity-inducing headlines practically force you to read more. They suck you in like a chocolate whirlpool.

This doesn't mean your book title has to be amazing. But it has to be focused on one benefit that the reader will get.

The title also helps you focus while you write your book. For example, when I wrote my book *Find Your Passion: 25 Questions You Must Ask Yourself*, I came up with the title first. Once I had the title, the rest fell into place.

How to Come Up With a Title

The key to coming up with a great title is to write a lot of titles. When you work on your title, write as many as you can. Focus on volume instead of perfection.

I have other tricks up my sleeve, too. Let's have a look at them:

1. Look at Titles You Like

The first step I take is to look for inspiration. I browse through books on Amazon and I write down titles that seem to pluck the strings of my heart—that resonate with me.

When I have 5-10 titles that I like, I take a look at my list, and I start playing with them. I take parts from one title and blend them together with another to create my title.

Once I've brainstormed a few versions of my own, I often find that I come up with a completely unique title. The reason I collect titles and play with them is not necessarily to come up with a title right then and there, but to get my creative juices flowing.

I don't panic if I don't come up with a title right away, because I know that my subconscious is digesting the problem. Eventually it'll spit something out.

2. Make a Promise

The second key to a powerful title is to make a promise. You may be afraid of making a promise, because it puts you under pressure to deliver, but that's not something to run away from. It's something to embrace with open arms.

The more clear your promise is, the easier it'll be for you to write your book. For example, if you want to write a book on growing tomatoes, a few titles, or promises, could be:

How to Grow Juicy Tomatoes in 30 Days or Less
The Beginner's Guide to Growing Juicy Tomatoes
How to Grow Organic Tomatoes Indoors

See? There's nothing fancy needed. Just an old fashioned promise is all it takes. If you want to write a book on how to write faster, you could play with titles such as:

17 Steps to Doubling Your Writing Speed
How to Double Your Writing Speed
Double or Triple Your Writing Speed in 7 Days

I'm repeating myself as you can see, but I want to drill home that coming up with a title for your ebook doesn't have to be hard.

3. What Would You Like?

Another way to come up with a title is to notice what you resonate with. Ultimately, you want to attract readers that are like-minded, because they'll resonate with your writing. To do that, write what you would want to read.

Another way to look at it is: Write what you would have liked to read. Let's say you're teaching people how to grow tomatoes. You could write to a past version of you, a version that doesn't know anything about growing tomatoes, yet.

Pretend that you go back in time and ask yourself if you'd like the title of your book. Would it be relevant? Would you want to read it?

You can ask the past you anything. Let your imagination run wild.

Bonus Tip: Synonyms

After you've come up with a list of possible titles, play around with synonyms. You can type in a word on websites such as http://thesaurus.com/ and it will spit out a smorgasbord of alternatives for you.

An Example

Now let's take a few example from my own books. For my book *Find Your Passion: 25 Questions You Must Ask Yourself*, I kind of cheated, because I'd written a similar blog post on my blog before. I simply took the gist of my blog headline and made it into a book title.

For my book, *Write Blog Posts Readers Love*, I made a simple promise. To be honest, I was stuck on my title for a long time, and I just went with the best I had at the time, and that was it. It isn't spectacular, but it's clear and gets the job done.

My focus was on moving forward. I wanted to avoid getting stuck, while at the same time providing value. Some might argue that if I'd work longer on my titles, I'd sell more books. That may be true, but it doesn't bring me joy to work too much on them. I enjoy writing, so I write.

I focus on enjoying what I do, because enjoyment and excitement are the sources of my motivation. When I do what I love, my life, business, and writing flow, and that's what I value in life.

Mistakes to Avoid

One mistake you should avoid is trying to get too creative with your titles. When you're writing a how-to, or nonfiction, book, people want to know what it's about and how it can help them, so make your title clear. Or put another way, answer the question: What's in it for me?

Another mistake is perfectionism. I'm going to remind you again to do what you can with what you have. Do your best to come up with a title. If you can't, let your brain chew on it for a while.

If you still can't come up with something, put up what you think is the best title and move on. You will get better at this as you write more. If you truly think your title is horrible, ask for help.

Do You Need a Title Before You Start?

I rarely have my title set before I start writing my book, but what I do have is the promise and focus of my book.

For example, with this book my promise is to help you write a high-quality ebook without driving yourself crazy. While writing this book, I kept a file with different titles, but I didn't know the "one" until the book was nearly finished.

So I had a focus for my book. I didn't just start writing randomly. I knew that my book would be about helping you write an ebook.

Action Steps

Here are the action steps that will help you come up with the title for your book:

1. **Inspiration.** Look at book titles you enjoy. Gather 5-10 or more. This will give you an overview of what kind of titles readers are interested in. Play around with these titles and create your own versions. After a while, you will come up with your own ideas.

2. **Make a Promise.** Next, play around with making a promise. What will readers get out of your book? What's in it for them? Will they learn to grow tomatoes? Get rid of fear? Learn to jump higher? How long will it take? Is this a guide, process, or something else?

3. **Time Machine.** Next, imagine stepping into a time machine and visiting a past version of yourself. Ask that you if he/she would like the title you've been working on. If you don't have a title, ask them what title they would like. What

would be relevant for them? Do they have any tips?

In the next chapter, you will learn how to find your ideal reader for your book, and why it matters. Ready?

3. Ideal Reader

An ideal reader is a person you hold in your imagination while writing your book. For example, when I was writing this book, I held one particular person in mind. He's a long-time reader of my work and I have spoken with him via email and Skype quite a bit, so I have a feel for his personality.

If you are writing for the first time, remember that you're not after perfection. You may have trouble coming up with an ideal reader. That's okay, and to be expected. All that is required is that you do your best.

In this chapter you will learn three ways to come up with your ideal reader, and by the end of this chapter, you will know enough to get started.

Reasons to Use an Ideal Reader

An ideal reader gives you focus, and it makes your writing flow better. It is as if you were sitting in a café chatting with a friend about a topic. You don't run out of things to say, because he or she keeps asking questions and making comments.

You write faster, because you no longer worry about whether or not people will criticize you. Okay, in reality, you will worry, but not as much.

You don't want to write for anyone and everyone. You want to write for your ideal reader, because there are plenty of people like your ideal reader in the world, and when they find one of your books, they will love it, because they will feel like it was written exclusively for them.

Having an ideal reader will also help you stay on topic, because you will be focused on helping your reader move forward.

How to Come Up with Your Ideal Reader

Coming up with your ideal reader is not as hard as it seems. You may feel like you can't imagine or visualize, but you can. If you can imagine what your living room looks like, you can do it.

And please, don't imagine a pink elephant flying across the sky with a black, velvet cape hanging from its back. See what I did there?

Now let's look at how you can find an ideal reader for your book.

1. A Friend

Imagine explaining the subject to a friend of yours. If I were completely new, I would imagine my partner. She's interested in new things and I know her reactions. If I were writing a book on growing tomatoes, I know she would be interested.

She likes gardening, but she doesn't necessarily know how to grow tomatoes indoors. Even if she did, I would imagine that she didn't. I would keep her in mind as I wrote my book, and I would pay attention to whether she became confused at any point. I am, of course, talking about the version of my partner in my imagination.

2. A Client

If you're a coach or consultant, pick a client or customer that you work with. Make sure you pick a client you like working with. You don't want any bad mojo getting in the way.

For example, as I mentioned earlier, I'm writing this book to one of my long-term readers. I don't always keep him in mind, because when I get into the flow, I just write what comes out of me. I know I can go back and edit and rewrite when I go through the book again, so it's not a big deal.

When I get stuck or confused, I bring my client to mind. It helps me get unstuck, and when it doesn't, I explore the problem through freewriting and get my subconscious on the job.

3. Past Version

Writing to a past version of you is another great way to create an ideal reader. For example, I was once afraid of writing. I was afraid of putting myself out there. I was uncertain about the future. I had all the fears we all have.

If I were to write a book about fears, I could write to the past version of me who is afraid and doesn't know what to do.

I would include a lot of personal stories that it's okay to be scared and that it's a learning opportunity. Writing to a past version of you is in some aspects the best way, because you know yourself so well.

And if you're writing your first book, writing to the past you is easy.

What If None of These Work for You?

If you can't come up with an ideal reader, then make one up. It doesn't matter. What matters is that you write.

If you can't figure it out, explore the problem with freewriting and try to solve it. Push yourself to the brink of frustration and turn it over to your subconscious mind. Write until you run out of steam and tell your subconscious: "All right, it's time for you to chew on this while I sleep and dream. Give me some clarity in the morning."

Then let it happen.

Example

I'm all over the place when I write my books. I don't adhere to rules if they don't feel right. What this means is that I'll keep an ideal reader in mind when I need to.

Other times I may simply let the outline of my book carry me forward. For example, I don't keep my ideal reader in mind while I'm writing this book. He pops in when I need him, and he goes out for a walk when I don't.

It's easy to believe that I've got it all together when I write, but I don't. Your favorite writers don't, either. They freak out. They get frustrated. They experience fear. They get stuck.

Everything you're experiencing is normal. What matters is that you don't let it stop you, but keep writing.

Mistakes to Avoid

You will have more than enough opportunity to rewrite and edit everything you write. When you remember that, you relax, because you don't have to get this perfect on the first go.

That's what I like about writing; it doesn't have to be perfect. I can write a horrible first draft. I can brainstorm as if I were insane, and I can put it all together when the time is right.

Don't get caught up in what you should do. Instead, focus on what you resonate with and what helps you move forward. Break the rules if you have to. But keep writing. Always keep writing.

Action Steps

The action steps for this chapter are simple:

1. Ideal reader. Who is your book for? Pick one of the three ways to come up with an ideal reader. If you want to, open up a new document and start exploring what ideal reader would be the best for you. Would a client work? What about a past version of yourself? Or even a person you know?

2. Good enough. Aim for good enough. Forget about perfection. You don't have to come up with the perfect ideal reader. I certainly don't. I keep one person in mind when I get stuck and when I outline my books.

3. Progress. Focus on constant improvement, not instant perfection. You may not love your writing, but that's because you want to improve. You have high standards, and that's a good thing. Don't stop writing just because you think you aren't great. There will always be room for improvement. Learn to love it, and learn to keep writing anyway.

Now let's move on to the creative brainstorm, which helps me write books faster, while reducing the overwhelm, stress, and struggle.

4. Creative Brainstorm

At this point you should have a vague idea of your:

- Intersection (where want and demand meet)
- Book title
- Ideal reader

It's time to do a creative brainstorm, which is all about creating a rough outline for your book. You see, your brain doesn't work in a linear fashion. Creativity doesn't happen in steps, it happens in chaotic bursts.

Where do solutions, ideas, and creativity come from? Some say from the ether, from the muse, while others say it's from the subconscious mind. I'd like to think that it's a mix, because we're interconnected to everything and everyone around us.

This chapter is about priming the pump. We're not trying to come up with a perfect outline for your book, instead we're going to play in the sandbox of ideas and see what happens when we travel to the edges of creative frustration.

I think you will find this new refreshing take, well, refreshing. Let's jump in.

What is a Creative Brainstorm?

A creative brainstorm means working with your brain and your subconscious mind. Most writers try to force their work. But I've discovered a better way.

You see, your subconscious is always at work. It takes care of everything from your heartbeat to how quickly your hair grows. It takes care of routine, so you can focus on new, important, and fascinating matters.

What most people don't realize is that your subconscious can help you solve problems and write books. An example of this is when you've been thinking about a problem for a long time. You struggle to an answer. You try and try until you give up in frustration.

And suddenly, while you're in the shower, the solution pops into your mind, like a cupboard door hitting you on the head when you least expect it.

Some people call this incubation. Here's how Wikipedia defines it:

"Incubation is one of the 4 proposed stages of creativity: preparation, incubation, illumination, and verification. Incubation is defined as a process of unconscious recombination of thought elements that were stimulated through conscious work at one point in time, resulting in novel ideas at some later point in time.

"The experience of leaving a problem for a period of time, then finding the difficulty evaporates on returning to the problem, or even more striking, that the solution "comes out of the blue", when thinking about something else, is widespread. Many guides to effective thinking and problem solving advise the reader to set problems aside for a time."

In short, a creative brainstorm is working with your whole being as it's supposed to be worked with. I rarely see authors talk about this, but it's crucial if you want to remain sane as a writer.

Reasons for a Creative Brainstorm

It takes the pressure off.

It primes your subconscious to help you with the writing process. In reality, your subconscious is always helping you. The question is: Are you cooperating?

You're quite literally going to play and experiment your book together. When I've done this, it's made my book writing process that much easier.

The times I've tried to force progress, I've run into trouble, and I've often had to rewrite the whole book anyway, so the path of least resistance works.

This doesn't mean you won't run into obstacles and fear, because you will, especially if this is your first book.

How to Brainstorm Creatively

So how do you brainstorm creatively, in a fun and enjoyable way? You tap into your childlike curiosity.

The more you suspend your fears, worries, and doubts, the more progress you will make. And don't worry. You will get better at this the more you do it.

Here are five things I do:

1. Write Your Title

Open a new document and write the title of your book at the top. If you don't have a title, write what your book will be about.

For example, if my book is about growing tomatoes indoors, the title would be *How to Grow Tomatoes Indoors*. I write that at the top of my document and proceed to step número dos.

2. Questions

Next, you answer a few questions through freewriting.

Freewriting to me means writing non-stop without editing. It means dumping my mind on paper.

The goal is not to come up with something remarkable. In fact, the more messy your freewriting, the better, because it's a sign that you aren't censoring yourself. You want to set your creative mind free and freewrite. If you want a good book on this, check out *Accidental Genius* by Mark Levy.

The first question to ask is: What will people expect when they see the title of this book?

Put yourself in your ideal readers' shoes and imagine what they think they will get out of your book. What will they expect from the title and focus of your book?

Once you've got the basics down of what they would like to know, ask yourself: What would delight my readers?

It might be sharing specific examples from your life in your book. It could be including one or two videos as a bonus. Get creative, but don't overstuff your book.

3. More Questions

Other questions I like to explore are:

- What goal do my readers ultimately want to reach?
- What steps do I need to cover in order to help them get there?
- What possible problems or obstacles will they face?
- What relevant and helpful stories can I share?

The first answer you get may seem obvious to you, but remember to dive deeper. Keep asking yourself why, how, when, where, and so on. Go deeper and deeper and challenge yourself to write more.

At some point, you will run out of things to write. When that happens, keep going, because you're on the verge of something great. Keep writing whatever comes to mind, even if it's about how much you hate me for making you do this.

4. Organize into Steps

Once you're done with freewriting, it's time to get a messy outline together. If I'm writing a book on how to grow tomatoes indoors, I'm going to think about what steps people need to take to grow tomatoes indoors for the first time. I'll start thinking step by step by step.

I don't know anything about growing tomatoes, but maybe the outline could look something like this:

Introduction
Why I Wrote This Book
How Tomatoes Have Helped Me
How to Read This Book
Finding the Best Equipment (for Cheap)
Finding the Right Seeds
Planting Your Seeds
Taking Care of Your Plants
When to Harvest
What to Expect
Mistakes to Avoid
Summary
About the Author

This is not a finished outline, but remember that we're exploring. I'm just writing this off the top of my head and seeing what comes out, because the deeper I dive into this, the more I'm priming my subconscious to help me.

The goal is to explore and *try* to come up with an outline. The mere act of putting in the effort will signal to your subconscious that this is important.

5. Let Go

Right about now, you might feel frustrated or confused. This is normal. It's a sign that something is going on under the hood. Don't worry. You're not trying to write a whole book right now or come up with perfect ideas. You're exploring.

At this point, I probably have a few pages with random, chaotic thoughts. I have a messy outline, and I may have other ideas written down. I'm not going to go in and fix anything right now, because I'm out of fuel.

I'm going to let go. Letting go is an essential part of allowing your subconscious to help you. Once you've done your creative brainstorm, your job is to take a break.

Example

With my book, *Follow Your Heart: 21 Days to a Happier, More Fulfilling Life*, my creative brainstorm was a mindmap. One day I got inspired to write a book on how to live a passionate life, or how I live a passionate life. I felt the urge to create a mindmap, so I opened up a (free) program called FreeMind and began mapping out the chapters.

I wrote down whatever came to mind. I had a working title, which ended up being my final title. From the title, I knew I needed to come up with 21 core chapters.

And I wanted those chapters to each be one of the biggest lessons in my life. I kept exploring and asking: What are the biggest lessons and realizations I've had that have helped me and still help me live a passionate, fulfilling, and happy life?

I then let go, and what I did next is coming in the next few chapters.

Mistakes to Avoid

Don't look for clarity too soon. You know you're trying to do something you can't do when you feel frustrated, overwhelmed, and lost.

There is no right or wrong way to do a creative brainstorm. The advice I've given you in this chapter is about how I start my creative brainstorm. Once I get going, I may invent new questions. I do whatever it takes to keep going and exploring.

This is about thinking hard about the problem (your book), and then letting go. When you do that, clarity will emerge. It may not happen all at once, although sometimes it does.

It's about letting your subconscious do the work for you as you sleep and dream. Your best decisions come out of the blue. You've probably noticed that, haven't you?

Action Steps

If you can use what you've learned in this chapter, it will not only change the way you write, but the way you live life.

Your subconscious is there to help you. It nudges you with inspiration all day long. It slips in solutions and makes you think you came up with them. Well, in reality, you did.

Here are the action steps for this chapter:

1. Title. Open up a document and write the title on the top of the page. You don't have to have a perfect title. If you don't have a title, write something that describes the focus of your book.

2. Questions + Freewrite. Ask questions, and explore them in writing, or in whatever way you feel comfortable. What will people expect? What kind of problems will they face? What are the steps to delivering on the promise of your book? What does your book need to contain in order to help your ideal reader?

3. Organize. Once you've done some freewriting and exploring, organize what you've found into steps. What are the steps people need to take in order to get to where they want to go? If I'm writing a book on growing tomatoes, I'll start thinking linearly and chronologically about what people need to do. I'll try to organize my chaotic (exploratory) writing.

4. Let Go. This is where the magic happens. Your creative brainstorm can feel like a failure, and it often should. It's a sign that you did proper freewriting and exploring. You will be rewarded, but you have to take a break. Leave your outline for a few days. If you want, you can return in a few days and explore further.

This is where the fun begins. Once you've gotten a creative brainstorm done, you can rest for a few days. When you're ready, we will create the blueprint for your book.

5. Book Blueprint

When I write, I do my best to structure and outline my book before I start. An outline keeps me on track. It keeps off-track writing to a minimum, which makes rewriting and revising faster.

In this chapter, I'll share my process for creating an outline for my book, or what I call a book blueprint. The process is simple, but it can take time for clarity to come for a visit.

Before we dive in, note that I use the words blueprint and outline interchangeably. To me, they mean the same thing.

Let's start.

What is a Book Blueprint?

A book blueprint is similar to a house blueprint. You don't start building without one, or at least, you shouldn't.

A book blueprint outlines the main chapters in your book. If you're writing a how-to book, they are often steps, such as the chapters in this book, which lead you step-by-step from A to Z.

Why Do You Need a Blueprint?

Writing by the seat of my pants doesn't work for me. Writing becomes easier when I blueprint my book before I start writing. I also experience peace of mind, because I can see (in my blueprint) whether I'm on track or not.

My blueprint ensures that I cover relevant content. This keeps my book focused and fluff-free. Readers love that, because they can read the same information faster.

Blueprinting also gives me an overview of my chapters before I start. This primes my subconscious for what's to come, and jumpstarts the problem solving machinery in my brain.

How to Blueprint Your Book

Blueprinting your book is about structure, as I mentioned above. Once you're done with your blueprint and chapter notes (more on this soon), your book almost writes itself. Let's look at the steps I take to blueprint my book:

1. Essentials

Every book has chapters and sections that need to be included, such as:

> *Copyright*
> *Table of Contents*
> *Introduction*
> *How to Read This Book*
> *Why I Wrote This Book (optional)*
> *Summary*
> *Additional Resources*
> *About the Author*

I start by throwing the essentials into an empty document. From there, I fill in the chapters. I use the above chapters in nearly all of my books. If you feel like adding or removing something, do it. Your book is yours. Use what I say as a springboard to your own ideas.

2. Chapters

From my creative brainstorm, I have raw material to work with. I take that material and hurl it into my outline.

For example, for this book, I asked myself: "What would the first step be for writing an ebook?"

The answer was: "How to come up with a topic that you are inspired to write about and that will sell."

Then I asked myself what step number two was. I kept going until I had most of my chapters. I've moved around chapters several times as I worked on the draft for this book.

I use Scrivener for writing my books. Scrivener makes moving chapters around effortless. We will talk more about tools and software in the formatting chapter.

In short, now is the time to create your table of contents—the main chapters of your book. Perfection is not required.

3. Reality Check

Once I have a messy blueprint in place, I ask: "Does this make sense?"

Put yourself in the shoes of your reader, and imagine going through the steps. Are there any gaps? What needs to be added or removed?

Watch out for bloat. I often want to add more than is needed. I want to make sure people like my book, but there's a fine line between providing value and giving into your fears (and overwhelming your reader).

Each chapter should contribute to the purpose of your book. Each chapter should move your reader one step forward.

An Extra Tip

When I'm at a loss for how to structure my book, I look at similar books in my topic area. I look for structure I can borrow. I'm not talking about plagiarizing, or even copying their structure. I'm after inspiration.

When I interviewed best-selling author Jennifer Louden, she talked about how she looked at her favorite books, and their structure, to get an idea for how to structure her book.

(If you're interested in listening to the interview, you can find it here: http://www.wakeupcloud.com/8/)

So go on Amazon, or visit your library, and look at books you like. How are they structured?

Example

In the last chapter, I showed you an example of a rough outline about growing tomatoes. Let's expand on that example here and see what we come up with.

Staying on the topic of growing tomatoes, I'll start with the essential chapters (copyright, introduction, summary, etc).

I'll look at my creative brainstorm and ask: "What's the first step someone needs to take to start growing tomatoes indoors?"

The answer might be: "They need to know what kind of tomatoes they need to grow."

As I keep asking myself what the next step is, I might come up with an outline like this (note that the essential chapters are included):

Copyright
Table of Contents

I threw this fictional outline together within a minute. I wrote down whatever came to mind.

Next, I refine the outline. I'd look at other books, and my creative brainstorm, and see if I'd forgotten something.

If the outline seems good, I proceed to blueprinting the chapters.

What If You're Still Confused?

Your blueprint may be messy at first, especially if you haven't written books before. This is where our house blueprint analogy collapses, because your book blueprint doesn't have to be perfect.

I know I keep repeating the fact that nothing has to be perfect. I repeat myself because I know you will try to get everything perfect anyway. How do I know? Because I do the same thing, but I've noticed that when I'm not in perfectionism mode, my book comes together without as much struggle.

While writing this book, I knew I'd be writing a step by step book, so I was confident that as I wrote, I would know what the next step, and chapter, would be.

If you're still stuck, the solution is movement.

When I get stuck, it's because I'm trying to come up with a perfect blueprint before I've started writing. When I lower the bar and write, I'm freed from the quicksand of stuckness.

Mistakes to Avoid

Beware of not starting at all. Refuse to stand still. Refuse to be stuck.

This is about coming up with the chapters for your book. You have material from your creative brainstorm. Start there, and start throwing together random ideas.

Don't look at this as writing a book. This is exploration. The more you shift how you view writing, the more effortless writing becomes.

Action Steps

We've reached the end of this chapter. Here's how you can implement what you've learned:

> **1. Essentials.** Open up a new document. Write down the essential chapters of your book. Add or subtract as needed. Perfection is not required. Throw something on the page so it isn't blank. It feels better that way.

2. Blueprint. Next, take a look at your creative brainstorm and jot down chapter ideas. Let it be messy. Let yourself be uncomfortable. Write down something, anything. It doesn't matter, because you can put them in order later.

3. Reality Check. Look at your book blueprint. Does it make sense? Is something missing? Does something need to be added? I like to stare at my blueprint and relax into it. It's kind of like daydreaming. I don't try to do anything, but I lazily think about if it could be improved.

Going through the motions will get your subconscious gears turning, even if you don't come up with anything. The act of thinking about something mobilizes your problem-solving troops.

In the next chapter, you will learn how to blueprint, or outline, each of your chapters.

6. Chapter Blueprint

The previous chapter was about creating a book blueprint—writing the main chapters for your book.

In this chapter, you will learn to blueprint your chapters. Once again, remember that your blueprints don't have to be perfect. It's more important that you move forward.

If you get stuck, lower your standards, and let your blueprints be what they are. Clarity will come.

What is a Chapter Blueprint?

The chapter blueprint is identical to the book blueprint with one difference: instead of outlining your book, you outline your chapters.

Imagine each of your chapters as a mini-book, or an article. As with the book blueprint, you will get a better overview of your book and where it's going when you blueprint your chapters.

Why is a Chapter Blueprint Important?

Outlining your chapters gives you a roadmap to follow. The outline keeps you on track, and saves time when rewriting and editing.

A chapter blueprint also gets the gears churning in your subconscious. Remember, the more effort you put in, the more you try, the more clarity will come (in time).

You will also see if what you want to cover in each chapter is relevant to your book. As you go through this process, you may discover that a chapter needs to be re-arranged, or removed altogether.

How to Create a Chapter Blueprint

So how do you create a chapter blueprint? Let's have a look.

1. Structure

A chapter blueprint starts with structure. When I'm outlining a book, I try to find a common structure I can use in each chapter.

For example, a simple chapter structure I like to use looks something like this:

(Note: The below structure holds subheadings for each chapter of my book. I try to use the same structure in each chapter. Sometimes it doesn't make sense, so the structure may be different in one or two chapters.)

What
Why
How
What If
Example
Mistakes
Summary (or Action Steps)

If you take a look at the structure of this book, you will see it follows this form.

2. Chapter Blueprint

Next, I turn the structure above into subheadings for my chapter. For example, the headings for this chapter are:

> *Introduction (not visible)*
> *What is a chapter blueprint?*
> *Why is it important?*
> *How to create a chapter blueprint*
> *1. Structure*
> *2. Chapter blueprint*
> *3. Reality check*
> *What if the structure doesn't fit?*
> *Example*
> *Mistakes to avoid*
> *Action steps*

This structure didn't pop out for me right away. It came from starting with the what-why-how structure above and asking questions, such as: What's the first step in this chapter my reader needs to know about?

At times it was as simple as plugging my concept or idea into the structure.

3. Reality Check

As with the book blueprint, I do a reality check once I'm done, I ask: "Does this make sense?" I go through the chapter again, reading it as if I was my ideal reader. With this chapter, it did, so I moved on to the next chapter.

Now, if you're anything like me, you like to complicate things. Pay attention if this happens, and remind yourself that your goal is to move forward. Your goal is to get somewhat of a blueprint done so you can start writing.

Sometimes writing a book comes easily to me, and sometimes it's like trying to write with a storm going on inside my head.

What If the Structure Doesn't Fit?

You don't have to force the what-why-how structure. I use it to get my outline going, and give me ideas. I quickly see if another structure is needed.

The structure is there to free you up, not to bind you down. Focus on your ideal reader and what would benefit them. What is the best way for them to take in what you have to share?

Example #1

Let me give you an example from my book, *Find Your Passion: 25 Questions You Must Ask Yourself.* In it, each chapter is a question, and before I started writing, I wanted to come up with a simple, common structure for each chapter.

The blueprint (or structure) for each chapter looks like this:

Introduction
Possible roadblocks
Time to write

That's it. Each chapter has a simple structure, and gauging from the feedback so far, readers love it.

Let me give you another example.

Example #2

In the last chapter, we created a book blueprint for my fictional tomato-growing book. Below I've taken the first few chapters to illustrate the chapter blueprinting process.

To refresh your memory, here's the book blueprint for the first three chapters:

1. Tomato Seeds
2. Equipment
3. Soil

And here it is with the chapter blueprint in place:

Chapter 1. Tomato Seeds
- What are tomato seeds?
- Why is it so important to pick the right one?
- How do I find the best seeds?
- Example: How I picked the right seeds
- Mistakes to avoid
- What to do next (action steps)
Chapter 2. Equipment
- What equipment do you need?
- Why is getting quality equipment essential?
- How to find the best equipment (for the best price)
- Example: How I picked my equipment
- Mistakes to avoid
- What to do next (action steps)
Chapter 3. Soil
- What is soil? (Soil explained)
- Why is the right soil important?
- How to find the right soil for your tomatoes
- Example: How I find good soil
- Mistakes to avoid

- What to do next (action steps)
Can you see how you can plug in the what-why-how structure to your book? If not, you may need another structure. For now, play with the what, why, how structure.

Mistakes to Avoid

Once again, perfectionism is your enemy. Relax when you create your chapter blueprints. Don't aim for perfection. Let it be messy. I know I'm being vague here, but you have to figure out what works for you.

For me writing is about being aware of the obstacles I put in front of myself. It's about realizing that I may always be anxious, but I don't have to stop just because I have a fearful or doubtful thought. I can keep writing.

The more you play, the more you allow your inner genius to say hi. So relax, play, and experiment. That's how your book will come together without the stress. You're still in the drafting and exploring phase. Remember that.

A Few Bonus Tips

To stay on track, write at the beginning of each chapter: What is the purpose of this chapter? How does it help fulfill the expectations I set in the book title?

If you want to get an even better overview of your book, put your outline in a mindmap.

The key to using the above structure is to cover just one concept or idea per chapter. For example, when you look at the table of contents of this book, you see one concept per chapter (most of the time).

Action Steps

That's that for this chapter. Here are your action steps:

1. Structure. Go to one of your chapters. Pick the one that feels easiest. Throw in the what-why-how structure.

2. Blueprint. Take the what-why-how structure and modify the subheadings to become your own. Make them fit with your chapter.

3. Reality Check. If you need to eliminate a part of the what-why-how structure, do so. Maybe you don't need the What because it's in the introduction. That's fine. Do what makes sense for you and use whatever parts feel good. Focus on your ideal reader.

We're ready to move to chapter notes, and when we're done with those, we will start writing.

7. Chapter Notes

You've got your book blueprint and chapter blueprints somewhat done. Or, if you're like most people, you're just reading through this book and you haven't done anything, but let's pretend that you have.

With an outline in place for both your book and your individual chapters, there's only one step left, and that is to throw in notes under each subheading in each chapter.

Don't worry if this doesn't make sense. In this chapter you will learn everything you need to know about chapter notes and how they work.

What Are Chapter Notes?

Imagine that you're taking a walk and you come to a large river. There is no bridge, but there are stones you can hop on to get to the other side.

Chapter notes are like those stones. When you write them, you create stepping stones that you touch. You write from one stone to the next.

Here's an example of my notes for this subheading (What Are Chapter Notes?):

> ### *What Are Chapter Notes?*
> *- Stepping stones across a river*
> *- Chapter notes are like those stones (make it easy to write)*
> *- Example of chapter notes*

That's it. Just three quick stepping stones to show the way.

Why Are Chapter Notes Important?

Chapter notes help you stay on track. You plan before you write, because it leaves more energy to focus on writing.

Writing down notes under each subheading in each chapter also gives you an overview of whether or not you're heading in the right direction.

If you're blueprinting your book in a mind map, you get a complete overview of chapters, chapter subheadings, and chapter notes. You can easily move things around.

Last but not least, chapter notes give you room to explore as you write from one note to the next (remember the stepping stone analogy). It's fun, productive, and you don't end up with writer's block.

How to Use Chapter Notes

Writing chapter notes is as easy as gobbling up a box of Belgian chocolate, and it's almost as delicious, because you're not trying to write anything, you're simply jotting down thoughts.

The way I use chapter notes is to write down notes under each sub-heading in each of my chapters. I don't do this all at once. I take my time. I remind myself that there's no rush. I can enjoy the process.

The idea with notes is to—as I've been repeating over and over—write down whatever comes to mind. Don't censor yourself, but write down ideas that might be relevant to that subheading.

Example

I've already given you an example of what chapter notes are, but I know this can be confusing, so let me give you an example of a whole chapter with notes.

This example is from the next chapter in this book (Chapter 8: Horrible First Draft). Pay special attention to how casual my notes are.

Here's the example:

Introduction here. Don't know what it'll be yet. I'll know when I write the preceding chapter.
What is a Horrible First Draft?
- Freewriting
- Writing without editing
Reasons to Write Horribly
- Helps you write a better book if done right
- Helps you write faster
- Makes it more fun (once you get used to it)
How to Write Your First Draft
- Outline/blueprint in place
- Start with easiest chapter to get into flow
— As you write more, you'll get ideas and things will fall into place
- Freewrite (use pomodoro if need to)
- Keep Writing (in the beginning you'll inevitably run into resistance and feel like it's not good enough, but remember this is not the book you'll publish. You're freewriting because this will help you write a better book. The editor and writer is not same part of brain.)
- Ask questions
What If Run Out of Things to Write About?
- Just write something
- Even bla bla bla is fine
- Keep going

Example
- *I was confused*
- *I decided to just write as I so often have better ideas by writing badly*
- *Gives my subconscious chance to work on it for a few weeks*
- *Same thing happened with my FYH book, I tried to force it, and then suddenly I woke up and trimmed 25% of the book effortlessly*
- *It's like oven goes ding when things are ready*

A Note on Research
- *If you write what you know, you won't need much*
- *If you do, leave gaps in your first draft, don't let it slow you down*

Mistakes to Avoid
- *Do not go into rewriting after your first draft is done*
- *Let it sit*
- *Biggest is to let your resistance/fears stop you from freewriting*

Action Steps
1. Start with easiest chapter
2. Freewrite
3. Ask questions

Not all of the above notes will make it into the actual chapter, but I still wanted to show you the raw format of my notes, because as you can see, your notes do not have to be perfect.

Mistakes to Avoid

I'm going to harp once again on the fact that you should avoid perfectionism. This whole blueprint process (book, chapters, notes) is about writing down whatever comes to mind. No censoring allowed.

When you start writing, you should write without stopping, because it is when you're relaxed that your inner genius says hi.

Even though I know all this, I still censor myself. I push myself too hard. I think my writing should be better. It seems to be a part of being a writer.

Action Steps

Here are your action steps for this chapter:

1. Start Easy. Find a chapter that you feel inspired to work on.

2. Notes. Jot down a few notes under each subheading. Lower your standards. Let it be messy, and write whatever comes to mind. You will edit later.

3. Relax. Remember to relax. I'm going to repeat this one more time: Relax. Have fun and experiment. The more you let go, the more you allow your inner genius to fill in the blanks.

When you're done with chapter notes, it's time to write your first draft. Your *horrible* draft.

8. Horrible First Draft

You've got your book blueprint, chapter blueprints, and chapter notes in place. It's time to write.

When my blueprints and notes are in place, my writing is more effortless. But sometimes my outlines aren't perfect. During those times, I do my best. I write a first draft despite the confusion I feel.

You don't have to feel good about your writing in order to write a good book. That's why this chapter is about writing a horrible first draft.

Forget perfection, embrace progress. If you feel confused, lower your standards, and write anyway. Once your first draft is done, your subconscious will have more to work with.

What is a Horrible First Draft?

A horrible first draft means writing like you're insane. It means writing without looking back. It means letting things get messy—as messy as a room full of toddlers with buckets of paint.

It's also called freewriting. Here's how Wikipedia defines freewriting:

> *"Free writing is a prewriting technique in which a person writes continuously for a set period of time without regard to spelling, grammar, or topic. It produces raw, often unusable material, but helps writers overcome blocks of apathy and self-criticism."*

While Wikipedia seems to think that freewriting produces mostly unusable material, I will have to disagree. If you freewrite without blueprints in place, you will end up with a lot of, well, crap.

But write with your blueprints and outlines in place, and you're armed with a weapon that will not only help you write your book faster, it will also allow your inner genius to come sit beside you.

Reasons to Write Horribly

Writing fast is hard. It feels like I'm doing something wrong. It was worse in the beginning, but I've grown accustomed to the feeling. I've learned that my book has to be messy before it comes together.

Writing horribly is also more fun than trying to write perfectly right away. As I write this, I let the words flow without worrying about what you might think or what might happen. Granted, it's not easy, but it's the only way I can stay sane.

Sometimes I'm surprised by how good my horrible first draft is. And sometimes I'm horrified at the gibberish I've produced. It's all okay, because the aim of my first (horrible) draft is to dump my mind on paper.

The goal is to write out everything relevant that I can come up with, and to keep writing until I'm done with my first draft.

How to Write Your First Draft

Before you start freewriting, you should have your blueprints and notes in place. Not perfect ones, but an outline that keeps you on track.

Here's how I write my first draft:

1. Write Without Stopping (Freewrite)

The goal is to write without stopping. I'll open a chapter, have my blueprint and notes in place, and start writing. I don't care where I start. I might start in the middle, or at the end. I pick something easy. I just want to get started, because I know starting is the hardest part.

I keep writing until the chapter is done. I don't care about sentence structure, flow, or grammar. My goal is to fill the chapter with words.

I may discard most of the words later, but what will remain are a few golden nuggets I can work with, and they will make my rewriting and editing easier. The more material I produce, the more I have to work with when I edit.

The key is to write. This chapter is about me trying to get you to write your chapter without editing. Freewriting isn't easy (at first), but you get used to it, and then you go, "Ooh. So this is what Henri was talking about."

2. Ask Questions

If I get stuck, I ask questions. So in this subheading, if I were stuck, I would start asking:

What is it about asking questions that works?
Why are questions important?
How on earth do you ask the right ones?
Any examples?
Mistakes?
What if no questions come to mind?

Do you also notice that I use the same what-why-how structure in my questions? I cover all the bases and eventually hit upon a question that gets me rolling again.

Remember, the goal is to keep writing. Let your first draft be horrible, but keep writing. When you ask the right questions, it's like the question magnetizes the answer and it bubbles up to the surface of your mind.

3. Get a Timer

If I'm scared, confused, or having a hard time getting my butt in the chair, I'll get a timer and set it for 20-25 minutes. I set my timer and I'll do nothing but write during those minutes.

This is also called the Pomodoro Technique, which you can learn more about by doing a search online. It has been proven to increase productivity, because when you work with a mini deadline, you become focused.

It's also easier to eliminate distractions because you know that you only have to write for 20 minutes, or whatever time you choose. So if you have trouble writing, grab a timer, and go.

What About Research?

When you write about what you know, you won't need to do a lot of research. If you still feel like it's relevant to your book, leave gaps in your first draft. Leave notes to yourself in places that need further research.

For example, if I were to put a note to myself here, it might look something like this: Remember to quote that brain research piece from New York Times to give proof about how your brain has superpowers.

Don't get stuck on doing the research, writing, doing the research, and jumping back and forth. Your goal is to get your first draft done. Research and editing comes later.

Mistakes to Avoid

The biggest mistake you can make when writing your first draft is stopping to edit, or research, or whatever your pet distraction is.

My mind is a master at coming up with reasons for why I don't have to write. I have to be vigilant, because if I'm not, I end up watching puppies on YouTube.

At times writing my first draft is a breeze, and at other times it's agony. Good or bad, I keep writing, because it is only through finishing my first draft that my book moves forward.

Just. Keep. Writing.

Action Steps

That brings us to the action steps for this chapter.

1. Start Easy. It's okay to pick the path of least resistance. When I start writing my book, I start with the chapter that feels the easiest. I'll keep writing and filling in the blanks until my first draft is done. Find your own way. Whatever you do, get that first draft done.

2. Freewrite. Once you've chosen a chapter, start writing, and don't stop. Freewriting may feel weird at first. It may feel like losing control. It's okay. It's normal. Just. Keep. Writing.

3. Ask questions. If you get stuck, turn your chapter headings and notes into questions. Put yourself in the shoes of your ideal reader and ask questions. Freewrite 20 questions. One of them is bound to get you going.

Next we will cover germination, which took me several years to discover, but once I did, it improved my writing dramatically, without any extra effort. Interested? Turn the page.

9. Germination

You learned about the concept of letting go in Chapter 4: Creative Brainstorm. In this chapter, we're going to apply the same concept to your book, but in a larger way.

For my books to turn out well, I need to give them time to rest. When I do, I give my subconscious mind the opportunity to work on them.

Let me give you an example of what I mean...

Have you ever tried to solve a problem but couldn't? You wondered if you'd ever be able to solve it. Then you gave up in sheer frustration. You didn't think about the problem for a while and suddenly, out of the blue, the answer came to you while driving, doing dishes, reading a book, or taking a shower.

That's your subconscious mind at work. Solutions pop up when you've put in the effort and try to solve them.

What is Germination?

Here's what Wikipedia says about germination (they use the term incubation):

> *"Incubation is defined as a process of unconscious [subconscious] recombination of thought elements that were stimulated through conscious work at one point in time, resulting in novel ideas at some later point in time.*
> *"The experience of leaving a problem for a period of time, then finding the difficulty evaporates on returning to the problem, or even*

more striking, that the solution "comes out of the blue," when thinking about something else, is widespread. Many guides to effective thinking and problem solving advise the reader to set problems aside for a time."

Germination, for me, is about working hard on my book, and pushing myself to the brink of frustration, and letting go.

Why Does Germination Matter?

Germination gives my subconscious time to put everything together. It makes my life easier, because I step into the boat, and ride the river of creativity. I realize that I can't force results, so I take a step back, and let everything come together in its own time.

I tried to force my books in the past, and I ended up with okay results, but not without struggle. I spent weeks trying to figure things out, and then suddenly things clicked. They clicked not because I was trying and thinking, but because enough time had passed.

It's like making a delicious lasagna. You put it in the oven and wait. It has to be in the oven for a certain amount of time. You can agonize over it. You can open the oven door, but it won't help. It will be done when it's done.

This is what germination is about—letting the lasagna become ready, while you take a break.

How Long Does Germination Take?

For me it's anywhere from a few days to a few weeks. For a book of about 15,000 words, 1-2 weeks seems to do the trick. This may be different for you. You have to experiment. I know the "lasagna" is ready when I feel fresh about my book.

For example, with my book *Follow Your Heart*, I felt confused while writing my first draft and while working on my second draft.

When I let it rest for two weeks, I came back and could easily see how to make the book better. I ended up removing 25% of the material and re-organizing a few chapters and it was easy.

How to Let Your Book Germinate

The germination process is not only effective in creative endeavors, but in anything and everything in life. If you're making a decision, think hard and deep on it first. Think about the options. Try to solve it, but once you reach the point of frustration, let go.

Let's look at how I use germination to write my books:

1. Plan Accordingly

The worst thing you can do is try to finish your book within a week, leaving no time for it to sit in the oven.

When I write my books, I try to plan for 1-2 weeks of germination time. For example, while writing this book, I had another book in the oven, waiting. After I finished the draft for this book, it went in the oven, and I started working on my next book.

2. Follow Your Interests

While my books sit in the oven, I do something else. It doesn't matter what I do. What matters is that I don't work on my book. At least not that specific book. If you want, you can work on another book (like I do from time to time).

In my case, if I'm not writing a book, I go about business as usual. I run an online business, and a blog over at Wake Up Cloud (http://www.wakeupcloud.com/), so I have plenty to do.

3. Listen to Inspiration

During the germination process, I get bursts of inspiration. These bursts are a sign that my subconscious is working on my book.

When I experience these lightbulb moments, I jot them down, and I throw them in a relevant chapter.

For some books, I won't get any inspiration until I start working on my second draft, so don't worry about what this process looks like for you. Whatever happens, happens. Just keep writing.

What If You Have a Deadline?

You plan. Deadlines are good when writing books, because germination can turn into procrastination if you're not careful.

For example, if you know you have 90 days to write a book, or finish something, you can plan backwards. The more books you write, the more accurate you become at knowing how long it will take you. Now, it's impossible to know exactly, but you can guess.

When I guess, I throw in buffers of time. Meaning, I overestimate how long it will take me. But just because you have a deadline doesn't mean you have to rush, or eliminate germination. It just means that you have to plan for it.

Mistakes to Avoid

The biggest mistake you can make is to not let your books germinate.

The other mistake is to stress out about how your subconscious works. Your brain will work differently from mine, so your germination process may be shorter, or it may be longer.

It doesn't matter. What matters is that you learn your own patterns. The way I figured out my germination patterns was by observing what happened. I stumbled all over the place and accidentally discovered what worked.

You may feel a sense of unease leaving your book unfinished for a few weeks, but remember, letting your book germinate is part of the process towards finishing it.

Further Reading

If you want more information on how your subconscious mind works and how to use it to create the life you want, and write great books, I highly recommend the book *Psycho-cybernetics* by Maxwell Maltz. It's a classic, and well worth the read.

Action Steps

Here are the action steps for this chapter:

1. Plan. When will you let your book rest? I let my books sit in the oven after my first horrible draft. That's when I've put in the effort and waded through enough confusion for my subconscious mind to kick in. The more books you write, the more you will uncover what is right for you.

2. Inspiration. As your book germinates, capture your inspirational bursts. When you get home, throw your bits of inspiration into relevant chapters.

3. Enjoy. Last, but not least, remember to enjoy the writing process. You write because enjoy it, so don't take your book too seriously. Don't take life too seriously. You're here to enjoy life, not to agonize over every little detail.

When the oven goes ding, and your book is done, it's time to move on to the second draft, which is where we start polishing your book.

10. Second Draft

The second draft is all about tidying up the mess I created in the first (horrible) draft.

I go through my book sentence by sentence, paragraph by paragraph. I remove the superfluous, and add clarification where needed.

I find working with a second draft much easier, because I'm no longer staring at a blank page. I have something to work with, something to mold.

Reasons to Write a Second Draft

Using the three-draft system takes the pressure off. I write a first horrible draft. Then I write the second draft, where I make my book readable. Finally, I write a third draft where I go through the finer details.

In each draft, I focus on as few details as possible, which minimizes overwhelm, because when I try to do everything in one go, my brain explodes. It's like trying to pour a bucket of water into a cup.

How to Write a Second Draft

For the second draft, my goal is to make my book somewhat comprehensible. While the first draft may not be understandable to outsiders, the second draft is. Readability is my only goal.

I'm after improving my book. If I try to get it perfect, I get stuck, and no progress is made.

Here's how I write a second draft:

1. Rewrite

When I open my first draft, I start rewriting wherever feels best. It's rarely the introduction, or the first chapter, but often somewhere in the middle of my book.

I start by reading from top to bottom. What I'm looking for are places where I can say something better, remove something, or add clarification.

I put myself in the shoes of my ideal reader, and I imagine that I'm reading my book as my ideal reader— someone who may not know much about the subject matter.

2. Edit

The next step is to edit, which to me means tweaking words and correcting typos. This happens while rewriting, mainly for sentences that don't need any large tweaks.

All in all, this is a simple process. The trick lies in doing it. I don't have a magical formula. All I do is go through my book and try to make it better for my ideal reader.

3. Simplify

Third, the goal of my second draft is to simplify and clarify. All of the three points I've covered here are really the same point, but I wanted to break them apart to give you a better view of what goes on in my head.

When you have the underlying goal in place, everything becomes easier. And what is that underlying goal you ask? It's about guiding your ideal reader to their goal.

If I'm writing a book about growing tomatoes, I want to make it as clear and simple as possible. I want to make sure I've done my best to delight my reader.

Example

Let me give you a brief example of how I edit. Here's a fictional paragraph in first (horrible) draft format:

> *"If you want to write a good book, you have to write a lot, and you have to think in the right ways. You have to use your unconscious to cooperate with you. But above all you have to be willing to face your fears and trust what comes through your fingers."*

Here's what it would look like after I'd gone through it for the second draft:

> *"The key to writing good books is to write a lot, using your subconscious, and facing your innermost fears. There's no magic involved. Just good old fashioned determination."*

As you can see, the second draft version is simpler and more to the point. In the first draft, I wrote whatever came to mind.

I'm not too concerned about getting my second draft perfect, either. I do my best, and if something isn't immediately clear, I'll think about it, and leave it for the third draft.

Mistakes to Avoid

The mistake I run into with my second draft is trying to polish too much. When I find myself staring at a paragraph for too long, I know I'm trying too hard.

The second draft is about light polishing. It's not about getting your book publish-ready.

For me, the second draft is about rewriting and making what my first draft was readable. The third draft is about polishing and making my book publish-ready before I send it to my editor.

Action Step

The only action step for this chapter is to begin. Open up your book at whatever place you feel is easiest and start rewriting. Read a paragraph and see if you can reword it. Try to say the same thing in fewer words. Put yourself in your reader's shoes, and try to make it better and more concise.

Once you're done with your second draft, we move on to the final draft.

11. Final Draft

The third draft is often my final draft, but I still tend to go through my book one more time before I hit publish. I want to make sure everything looks right.

So my last read-through isn't necessarily a draft. It's me reading through the book. If I find errors, I'll correct them, but usually things look good.

This chapter is short and to the point, because you already know what to do.

There are no rules to writing. You have to make up your own rules. I break my writing into three drafts because it makes it easier for me to write books. I like structure.

Sometimes I break my own structure. I may do more drafts. I may do less. I go with what feels best in the moment.

What is a Final Draft?

A final draft is where I get nit-picky. I look for grammar errors and I do a run through of my book before sending it to my early feedback readers, and my editor.

My final (or third) drafts are fairly uneventful. Sometimes I'll find something that needs a complete rewrite, but more often than not, I end up tweaking a few words here and there.

Reasons to Write a Final Draft

The third draft is all about making sure that there are no glaring errors left unfixed.

If there are, it's not a problem, because I'll send my book to people who will give me feedback. After that, I'll send my book to an editor who will spot any remaining mistakes.

I've learned to think of writing my third draft to good enough—to 80% done. It helps keep perfectionism at bay, and instead of writing in the dark, I can rely on feedback from real people.

How to Write a Final Draft

In the final draft, I allow myself to dip my toes in perfectionism. I rarely find anything big that needs changing, so I'm mostly reading through and looking for small tweaks I can make.

I look for words that aren't clear. Sentences that could be removed. Paragraphs that could be shortened. Anything ambiguous that might leave my ideal reader confused.

My goal is the same as it was in the second draft: to clarify and simplify. I know I won't catch everything, and that's fine. My goal is not to try to write the perfect book, but to get it good enough.

I never feel like my books are 100% done. I've realized that the feeling of inadequacy doesn't mean my books aren't done. In other words, just because I feel like a book isn't done doesn't mean it's not done.

You may want to read that again.

Your Subconscious is Still Working

As I go through my drafts, I get ideas. The ideas don't stop. My subconscious is still hard at work, so lightbulb moments happen even as I'm finishing my book.

The more time I let pass between my drafts, the easier it is to rewrite and edit. So when you're working on your book, take it easy. Go slower than you think you can. Get one draft done and take a break.

Mistakes to Avoid

Avoid taking my writing process as law. Your writing will differ from book to book. Be flexible and stay focused on the main goal, which is to write the best book you can write, without trying to reach perfection.

As you write more, you get better. You notice subtle nuances. Remember, Stephen King has been writing for years. He didn't just pop out of the womb with a pen in his hand. He had to write a lot, and read a lot.

So write, face your fears, and hit publish.

Action Step

There's only one action step for this chapter: To read through your book and make any final adjustments.

You may feel like your book isn't good enough. Every writer feels that way. But get it to 80% done and send it away.

To whom? That's what we will cover next.

12. Getting Feedback

Your final draft is done, or it feels 80% done. There may still be parts that don't feel done, and that's okay. That's how you're supposed to feel when you send your book out to get feedback.

With my first few books, I didn't want to send my book to anyone before I felt 100%. I've since changed my tune, because I'm much more productive when I get my book to good enough, and then get feedback.

Getting feedback from real people relieves stress, because I don't have to try and figure everything out. It's easy for me to get stuck in a vicious cycle where I feel like something is wrong without knowing what it is.

What is Feedback?

Feedback is letting other people tell you what they think about your book. I'm not talking about giving your book to just anyone, but to people who can give constructive criticism. For me, these are my blog readers, students, and clients.

Different people will give different kind of feedback. Some will tell you about grammar and typos. Others will focus on how different chapters feel, while yet others will tell you what steps are missing and what parts are confusing.

Getting feedback shows you that what you think is wrong isn't always wrong, and what you think is right isn't always right. You uncover ideas you may not have thought of. It's not even necessary to take the feedback literally, because what you get back may serve as a springboard to new ideas.

Reasons to Get Feedback

I get feedback to ensure that my book is good enough to publish. I tend to worry, so getting real people to read my book and tell me what they think helps.

Feedback confirms that I'm on the right track. I can always improve my writing, so I'll invariably get feedback on what I can do better. If you're just looking for people to tell you that you're awesome, your priorities are wrong.

Getting feedback is also a faster way of writing a book, because I don't have to figure everything out. I can do my best, send out copies, and see what people think.

How to Get Feedback

Getting feedback may seem scary, but it's the fastest path to seeing what readers think of your book, and what you can do to improve it.

Here's how I go about getting feedback:

1. Find People

The first step is to find people. I have an existing audience with my blog, Wake Up Cloud, and I have a presence on social media, so I use what I have to ask people for feedback.

What if you don't have an audience? No problem. Find forums in your niche. Find blog owners and ask them if you can give their audience a free book in exchange for feedback. Look for Facebook groups. The key is to find people who are genuinely interested in your book.

Once you've found 6-12 people that are interested in not only reading your book, but giving feedback, send them your book.

2. Expectations

Next, set the right expectations. Tell people what kind of feedback you want. Do you want them to spot typos or grammar errors, or do you want something else?

Here's what I tell my feedback readers:

"This is a rough draft, so you may find grammar errors, awkward flow, and typos. If you do find them, I'd love it if you could point them out. I'd also like it if you were completely honest with me as you read the book. In other words, I'd like to know if you think something is missing or if something should be removed. I want to make this the best book possible, so be honest with me."

When you set the right expectations, you get better results than a vague: "Give me some feedback. Thanks."

3. Drill Deeper

Once your feedback readers tell you what they think, you have to be willing to drill deeper. People tend to be very general when giving feedback, and they assume you know what they are talking about.

Here's an imaginary conversation with an example of the feedback I sometimes get:

Reader: I really liked the chapter about the kind of seeds you need to buy to grow tomatoes indoors, but I was confused.
Henri: What were you confused about? Could you be more specific?
Reader: I was confused about where to find the seeds. I know there are stores, but there are so many tomato seeds to choose from.
Henri: Aha, would it help to have the exact name of the seeds in the book that tell you what to look for in different situations?
Reader: Yes, that would be perfect. Thank you!

Get into what specifically they are confused about. Once you know, suggest a solution that you think fixes the problem and ask them if you're on the right track.

You won't always be able to fix everything, but you can do your best. Remember, your book doesn't have to be the ultimate guide to anything.

Example

When I had finished my third and final draft for my book, *Write Blog Posts Readers Love: A Step-By-Step Guide*, I felt confused. The book didn't feel good to me. It felt off, but I couldn't put my finger on it.

I decided that I'd done my best. I got in touch with a few readers from my audience and asked if they'd be interested in reading the book and giving me feedback. They said yes. I sent the book over.

When I received the feedback, I realized that my book didn't have enough examples. And in other places, the examples were confusing.

I had several a-ha moments, and I proceeded to put in examples and add several thousand words to the book. Once I was done, the book felt good, and I sent it off to my editor. I also sent a revised copy to one of my reviewers to ask him if things looked good. He gave it a thumbs up.

Mistakes to Avoid

I avoid pressuring people. Not everyone I send my book to will give me feedback. They may have over-promised, or maybe they don't feel inspired to read my book. That's okay. I leave them alone. I may remind them once, but if I don't hear from them, I let it go. I focus on the people who are interested.

The next mistake is to take the feedback personally. Learn to discern between feedback that is useful and feedback that is not.

Pick and choose the feedback you get so that you don't change your whole book to fit someone else. The changes you make have to make sense for you, and you have feel good about it.

Action Steps

We've reached the end of this chapter. Here are your action steps:

> **1. Find the Right People.** Use forums, blogs, social media, or whatever makes sense to you. Find 5-10 people that would like to read and give feedback on your book.

2. Expectations. Give your early readers something to focus on. What do you want them to give you feedback on? Are you worried about the structure? Tell them. Not quite sure if you've given enough examples? Ask them.

3. Specifics. Once you receive feedback, make sure you ask follow-up questions. Propose solutions and ask if you're on the right track.

After you've gotten enough feedback, go ahead and make the necessary changes in your book. When you're done, it's time to work with an editor and put in the finishing touches.

13. Working With an Editor

So you've gotten feedback, you've tweaked your book, and you're starting to feel good, or at least not horrified with your work.

You may still have worries and fears. That's normal. We're writers, after all. We freak out and we have visions of the world laughing at our writing and burning us at the stake.

That's why we have one more buffer in place—the editor. Your book is good, but you're not sure how good.

What is an Editor?

An editor is a confidence booster. My editor does the final check on my book. I'm not a native English speaker, and although my English is good, I want to make sure I minimize mistakes.

There's nothing more annoying than reading a book and bumping into typo after typo, or awkward sentence structure. A good editor helps you avoid that.

Do You Really Need an Editor?

You don't need one, but I highly recommend it, especially if you want to publish your book on Amazon. An editor doesn't have to be expensive. You can get a fairly standard copyedit done to check for grammar and typos for a few hundred.

If you publish your book to your own audience, that's a different matter. For example, I can launch an ebook or a course to my audience before it's finished as long as I set the right expectations. I can offer a discount in exchange for feedback.

However, if you're putting your book on Amazon, readers will expect a finished product.

How to Find an Editor

Finding a great editor can be hit and miss. I find the people I work with through word of mouth. My current editor was recommended to me by an old friend of mine who used to coach me when I played poker.

Here are a few quick tips to help you in your search:

1. Ask

As I mentioned above, I found my editor through word of mouth. The problem with asking popular authors is that they tend to work with pricey editors. If you can afford an expensive editor, that's fine, you will probably get a lot for your money.

However, if you're just starting out, I recommend you ask beginning authors. You want an editor that is good, but that doesn't cost thousands.

2. Keep Price in Mind

When you get an editor, you have to remember that you're making an investment. If you get $2 per book on Amazon, and you spend $200 on an editor, you have to sell 100 copies to break even.

This doesn't mean you should skimp on your editor, but you want to find a balance. I usually get a copyedit and flow check done on my books. If you aren't familiar with what flow is, it's making sure that the book makes sense, that it flows well from chapter to chapter.

3. Marketplaces

You can also check out marketplaces such as Upwork.com, where you can find plenty of freelancers in different fields. Do a search for editor or proofreader.

You will get a list of possible prospects. You can gauge their work via their portfolio. You can send messages and ask questions.

You may need to go through a few different editors to find one you like. That's the name of the game. You search until you find.

Example: How I Work with My Editor

I work with Anna Paradox from AnnaParadox.com. She is experienced, she listens, and she's fun to work with. On top of that, she's very affordable.

My process looks something like this:

1. Write my first draft
2. Rewrite (second draft)
3. Edit and fix small things (third draft)
4. Send to early reviewers
5. Fix according to feedback
6. Send book to Anna

When I get my book back, I fix any remaining typos and errors, and the book is ready to be published. After all this, I usually do a quick read through to make sure everything looks good.

Mistake

The mistake to avoid is what I've already mentioned: Don't spend too much. With your first few books, keep things lean. You don't know how your book will sell. The important part is to keep writing books, and to write because you enjoy writing.

Action Steps

Here are the action steps for this chapter:

1. Ask. Ask beginning authors who their editor is, and if they wouldn't mind sharing him or her. Ask on social media. Ask on forums. Ask wherever it makes sense.

2. Price. The money you spend on your editor is money you have to make back, so find a balance between expenses and profit. It's not easy, but you get better as you write more books.

3. Marketplaces. Last, but not least, check out marketplaces like Upwork.com, where you can find hundreds upon hundreds of editors and proofreaders.

Now let's move on to designing your book.

14. Design

Your book needs a good cover. You could do it yourself, but unless you're a designer chances are that it will end up looking, well, not so good.

I'll keep this chapter short and sweet, because the same general principles apply here as did in the previous chapter on finding an editor.

What is Ebook Design?

When I talk about ebook design, I'm referring to the cover of your ebook. If you want to put your book up on online marketplaces such as Amazon, Barnes & Noble, and so on, your cover matters.

If you're going to sell your ebook through your website, your cover still matters, but maybe not as much, because you have more room to put in your sales copy and description. Your readers will also have established a connection with you, compared to Amazon where most people are new to your world.

Why is a Cover Important?

Your cover helps sell your book. People do judge a book by its cover. This doesn't mean you have to get a world-class designer. It means your book cover can't look horrible.

A cover grabs attention. It nudges people to find out more and read the title of your book. If the title of your book is enticing, they might read the description, and on it goes, until they're ready to buy your book.

How to Find a Designer

Finding a designer for your ebook cover is like finding an editor. The same general principles apply:

1. Ask

Have you noticed someone who self-publishes and has amazing covers? Shoot them an email and ask who does their covers.

Ask more than one person. Remember, you have to find someone where the price is right. And what is the right price? Only you can decide. I prefer anything between $100-300.

2. Fiverr

Fiverr.com is hit and miss. You can get a cover for $5, but sometimes you will have to go through several designers to find what you want.

As usual, being specific about what you want, giving examples, and sketches, helps. The best way to find reputable and talented graphic designers on Fiverr is to look for those that have plenty of good reviews. Seems obvious, doesn't it?

Look for good reviews, and take a look at their past work. If they don't have any examples of past work, look elsewhere. There's a category just for ebook cover designs, so have a look there.

3. Marketplaces

Last, but not least, as with finding an editor, you can find oodles of talented designers at marketplaces such as Upwork.com.

The procedure is the same, but instead of looking for an editor, look for ebook covers or ebook design.

A Design Tip

I've worked with many designers over the years on projects ranging from website designs to book covers. I've found that the more precise I am about what I want, the more satisfying the end result is.

So how can you be precise? Sketch and give examples. Look at what covers you like and resonate with, and start drawing on paper what your cover might look like. As with creative brainstorming, don't try to come up with the perfect cover right away. Play around with it.

Give your designer examples of covers you like, and sketch something to give him or her direction.

Example

Let me give you an example on my cover creation process.

I start by looking at covers and products online. Amazon is a good place to start. I then start thinking about the cover. I sketch loosely on paper.

Inevitably, my first few attempts are frustrating and unfruitful. But I know that my subconscious is working on it. The key is starting to sketch and trying to figure it out. As the days pass, and as I spend a few minutes here and there sketching, I'll get an idea.

Once I have an idea, I'll tell my designer what I want. I'll take a photo of my sketch and email it to him. I'll also send over 2-3 covers of published books that I like so he can get a feel for what I'm after.

I don't always love the covers I come up with, but by working with a competent designer, I can get to good enough, and that's all I need.

Mistakes to Avoid

The biggest mistake is, once again, overspending, followed by perfectionism. In design matters, my perfectionism tendencies tend to take over.

I've noticed that there's a gap between when I create something and when I consume something. It's what I call the producer-consumer gap. When I work on a design for myself, I see all the small details that no one notices, and it drives me crazy.

But when I consume or use a design, or watch a book cover, I'm not as concerned as long as it's clear, looks good, and resonates with me. I've learned to switch to this consumer perspective when I'm evaluating designs. It helps me avoid outright panic.

Action Steps

Here are the action steps for this chapter:

> **1. Ask.** If you find an author who has a book cover you like, ask them who did the design. Look around. Ask around. You will eventually find a good designer. I personally work with

Charlie from CharfishDesign.com, so you may want to check him out.

2. Fiverr. If you're short on cash, try Fiverr.com. You may have to go through several designs, but who knows, you may strike gold.

3. Marketplaces. And once again, check out marketplaces such as Upwork.com. They have plenty of designers waiting to help you.

Now let's move on to formatting your book.

15. Formatting

I'm going to come right out and say that I'm not a formatting expert. I learn the minimum to make my books look good. I keep things simple and learn more as I move forward.

When I first began writing ebooks, formatting confused me. I didn't know what to do or where to start.

Suffice it to say, I felt frustrated. The good news is that I eventually figured out what I needed, and I'm going to share with you what tools I use.

I'm not going to dive in-depth into formatting, because there's plenty of information out there once you know what you need to use.

What is Formatting?

When I talk about formatting, I'm referring to the inside of your book. For example, with this Kindle book, the formatting is the size of the text, the fonts, the subheadings, the table of contents, and everything you see as you read this.

In Kindle and other ebook readers, readers can change the size and typeface of the text, which means that you just have to focus on getting the basics right.

When I write Kindle books, all I do is open up a new document in Scrivener and start writing. I make my subheadings a few points larger, and I bold and italicize them, as you can see in the chapters of this book.

PDF books retain the size, typeface, and graphics, so it's more important to get your book looking the way you want it.

Getting the formatting right may seem tricky, but when you've done it once, you know how to do it a million times. Anything technical is frustrating in the beginning. Take things one step at a time. If you get frustrated, remind yourself that there's no rush.

Reasons to Format Well

If you're going to publish your book on Amazon, bad formatting will disappoint people, and that disappointment will lead to bad reviews, which in turn may affect your sales. So you want to make sure you format your books properly.

Good, clear, and consistent formatting also makes for a better reading experience, which means people are more likely to read, finish, and recommend your book to others.

How to Format Your Ebooks

There are two types of ebooks that I write: Kindle and PDF. Kindle books obviously go on the Amazon marketplace (and other similar sites).

The PDF books I create for ebooks, products, and courses that I sell through my own site, WakeUpCloud.com. Let's have a look at how I produce both.

Consistency

It's important that you are consistent throughout your book. The more consistency and structure, the easier it is for your readers' brains to focus on the words on the page.

So you need to be consistent with your heading and subheading styles, your paragraph font and spacing, and your numbered list styles.

When I write my books, I tend to use the default styles, which means that I simply open up Scrivener and start writing. If you want to change fonts, you can do so, but I recommend you go with a proven font, such as Times New Roman.

Formatting for Kindle

I've heard many people use Microsoft Word to format for Kindle, and that's fine. I haven't done that. But if you want to find out more about how to do that, you can do so here:
http://www.wakeupcloud.com/kindleformatting

I use a program called Scrivener to write and format my books for the Kindle. It's one of the best investments I've made as a writer. It is not only good at converting books into Kindle format, it also helps me write and organize my books.

Why is it so great? Because it allows me to easily re-arrange chapters, write down notes, and get out of my way when I write my books. But this isn't a book about using Scrivener. I just wanted to share that I highly recommend you try it out.

Scrivener is available for both PC and Mac. You can find it here: http://www.literatureandlatte.com/

They also have an active community and great support if you get stuck.

I don't get any compensation if you buy Scrivener. I love it so much that I recommend it. Once you get it, they have information on how to format your book in various formats.

Formatting for PDF

You have more control over the look of your pages in a PDF book. So, have consistent styles for headings, headers, and footers. For more information, refer to the Amazon web page listed above or to the books in the resource section below.

If you aren't writing for the Kindle and want to produce a PDF ebook that you sell via your website, I recommend you use Microsoft Word or Pages if you're on a Mac.

They both have convert to PDF features that make your life easy. All you have to do is write your book and make it look good. Then convert to PDF and you're done.

If you have an older version of Microsoft Word, you may need to download a plugin. You can find it by doing a Google search for "Microsoft Word Save As PDF Plugin." It should be one of the first few results.

Mistakes to Avoid

When it comes to formatting, don't settle for checking that your ebook looks good on one device. Try it on different devices, especially if you're going for the Kindle. Luckily, Amazon gives you an online reader where you can see what your book looks like on different devices.

If you're creating a PDF ebook, you can usually get away with just making sure it looks good on your computer. When you send off review copies, you will quickly hear if there are issues.

Resources

In addition to the Amazon website, there are two books you may want to check out on formatting. They are:

- *Building Your Book for Kindle* by Amazon
- *Publishing E-Books for Dummies* by Ali Luke

Action Step

Here are the action steps:

1. Breathe. Technology is frustrating. When you feel yourself stuck in a web of panic, take a deep breath, and relax. You don't have to learn everything all at once. Start by getting acquainted with the software that's out there.

2. Software. Get the right software. If you plan on writing more than one book, I recommend Scrivener, especially if you intend on publishing your ebook on Amazon.

3. Start with the Basics. As you've noticed in this chapter, I've kept things simple. That's because I like minimalist formatting. There's no need to do anything fancy. The focus should be on your words. Your formatting should make reading easier.

Now that we've gotten formatting out of the way, let's move on to pricing.

16. Pricing

In this chapter I want to cover how I price my kindle books, and why I price them that way. I haven't done much testing, I've simply used the price that feels the best for me.

That's one of the advantages of not having to squeeze every penny out of everything. I can take the unscientific approach and do what feels good, while keeping in mind what's best for my readers.

This doesn't mean my pricing won't change in the future. But right now, this is where I'm at and I hope this chapter will help alleviate some of the fears and worries you have around pricing that I had in the beginning.

My goal with this chapter on pricing, and the next one on selling, is to keep things simple. I don't want to overwhelm you with details. I want you to take action, because when you take action and get your book out there, you learn.

You learn what works for you, and what you like. Other books go into detail on pricing and things to consider, but I'm about writing books and learning from my experiences.

What is Pricing?

When I refer to price, I'm referring to the price you set in the Amazon store when you setup your Kindle book.

In some countries, the price will change depending on how much VAT/tax is added by Amazon. For example, a $2.99 book is $3.74 in Finland (where I am right now). There's not much you can do about this.

Why is Setting the Right Price Important?

If you set your price between $2.99 and $9.99 you get 70% royalty from Amazon. Anything below or above that gives you 35%.

So if you set your price at $0.99, you would get around $0.34 per sale. If you sell 100 copies, you would make around $34.

On the other hand, if you priced your book at $2.99 and sold 100 copies, you would make around $200. Almost 6 times the amount.

This doesn't mean you should price all of your books between $2.99 and $9.99. What it means is that if you're thinking about writing a short $0.99 book, you might consider expanding it and making it a $2.99 book.

How to Price Your Book

Before you consider price, think about what the purpose of your book is. Do you want it to generate leads for your business? Do you want to make money off of your books? Do you want it to act as an authority builder for your existing business?

Let's have a look at the different options.

1. $0.99

A book priced below $2.99 is great for sales. It's quite obvious, isn't it? The lower your price, the better it will sell in most cases.

If you just want sales and eyeballs, you can use your book to get more people to visit your website and maybe join your newsletter by simply having a free gift or offer at the beginning and end of your book.

You don't have to be pushy about it, but you have to ask people to take action. A $0.99 book can also be a great introduction to your books. For example, if you help people grow tomatoes, you could have a primer priced at $0.99, and have the next books in your series go into more depth and be priced higher.

You want to test this for yourself, because sometimes you will get as many sales at $2.99 as you would get at $0.99.

2. $2.99

I like the $2.99 price, because it is low enough to get a lot of people interested, but high enough to generate income.

I enjoy making an income from my books, because it allows me to write more books, so that's why I choose the $2.99 price point.

Your price will depend on what your purpose is and what people expect in your market. You can start at any price point and see how things go. Keep track of your sales, change your price, and see what happens.

3. $4.99-9.99

The higher price points are good for more in-depth books, or for building authority. I generally write books that are between 12,000 and 22,000 words. They are easy to read and to the point.

If you're writing a longer book, you may want to consider a higher price. Again, it comes down to testing and what you want to get from your book.

If you write short books like I do, start with the $2.99 price point. You could launch your book for free, or for $0.99, and then raise the price.

What If You Don't Sell on Amazon?

If you're selling to your own audience, pricing will depend on what you offer. If you're just selling an ebook, you're limited to a certain price range, unless you offer highly specialized and rare information (e.g. tips for making more money for insurance lawyers).

The upside to selling to your own audience is packaging. Instead of selling an ebook, you can add audio, interviews, worksheets, and even 1-on-1 coaching. The more value you add, the higher the price.

The downside is that most people don't have the audience to launch their own products. That means you have to first build an audience, which you should be doing anyway.

If you're starting out, start with Amazon. Write a $2.99 book, and go from there. You can't really do anything wrong. What matters is that you start, because when you start, you discover what works and what doesn't.

Mistakes to Avoid

When I created my first few digital products (on my own blog), pricing made me uncomfortable. I had beliefs about money that held me back, so I undercharged.

And if you're anything like me, you will tend to undervalue your books and products. Know that just because you think you don't have anything to share, doesn't mean you don't have anything to share. You merely THINK that you don't. There's a difference.

Now, you may not be the best writer in the world, but when you share your story, you share something of value. You have overcome obstacles. You have solutions to share. So tell your story with confidence, and above all else, write, because when you write, you improve.

Action Steps

Let's have a look at the action steps for this chapter:

> **1. Purpose.** What is the purpose of your book? Do you want to generate traffic and subscribers to a website? Then go with $0.99. Do you want to make money while still keeping the price accessible? $2.99 is an option. Do you want to write a full-sized book and build authority? Consider $4.99-$9.99.

> **2. Where?** Where are you going to sell your book? If you already have an audience, your own website is a viable option. But if this is your first paid book (or product), I would strongly consider Amazon.

> **3. Beliefs.** Be aware of your beliefs around money. You may feel yourself getting uncomfortable when it comes to pricing. You will tend to undervalue yourself. Know that your story has value. Share it with confidence.

Now it's time to move to our last chapter on selling your book.

17. Selling

So we've talked about design, formatting, and pricing. Now it's time to cover how to sell your book. Once again, I'm not an expert on selling. I have mostly utilized my audience at Wake Up Cloud (http://www.wakeupcloud.com/) to sell my books.

So what I recommend is that you build an audience and a platform. It's a long-term strategy, but it allows you to launch books, courses, programs, and services, more easily.

Learning how to sell a book is a book in and of itself, but I want to briefly touch on how I do things.

Writing a book and putting it up on Amazon, or your website, doesn't automatically mean your book will sell. It is a starting point, and it is the first step on your journey to becoming an author.

What Does Selling Your Book Mean?

In order to sell your book, you need to get the right people in front of your book. Sounds obvious enough, doesn't it?

If you want to make it as an author in this day and age, it's not enough to publish a book. You have to think about how you're going to sell it.

Selling means writing a book that people want, and getting the right people in contact with your book. This is why building your own platform is important. If you're writing your first book, you may not have huge success, but know that it's normal.

You start at the beginning, like everyone else. The ones who make it are the ones who are willing to keep writing and keep learning.

4 Tips for Optimizing on Amazon

Let's look at a few things I've picked up from publishing books via Amazon.

Remember, these are simple tips, and that's how it should be. If you haven't published a single book, your focus should be on getting a book out there and then worrying about the finer details.

1. Keywords

What you see other authors recommend is to use keywords in the title and description of your book.

Why? Because your book will show up in the search engines, and it will show up in Amazon search. That means it's wise to align yourself with the words people are searching for.

I have a background in search engine optimization, so I'm familiar with this topic. It comes down to finding words people are searching for (that aren't too competitive), and tailoring your title and description accordingly.

For example, my first book, *Find Your Passion: 25 Questions You Must Ask Yourself*, uses the keyword phrase (a term to describe two or more keywords): Find Your Passion.

I know from writing about that subject on my blog that it's something readers are interested in. I also discovered that it's a key phrase that is searched a few thousand times per month.

The way to find these keywords is to use a free tool called Google Keyword Planner. You can Google it and it should pop up right at the top. You will need to create an AdWords account to use the Keyword Planner. It's free, and you don't need to run ads to use the keyword tool.

2. Categories

The next step is to pick the right categories for your book. When you publish your book, you will have the opportunity to pick categories.

Look for categories that don't have stiff competition. For example, for my *Find Your Passion* book, I inspected other books on Amazon that helped people find their passion. I scrolled down to the Product Details section.

In there, I saw the Amazon Best Sellers Rank, which often includes categories. It looks something like this:

Amazon Best Sellers Rank: #50,930 Paid in Kindle Store (See Top 100 Paid in Kindle Store)

> #33 in Kindle Store > Kindle eBooks > Business & Investing > Careers > Job Hunting
> #50 in Books > Business & Investing > Job Hunting & Careers > Job Hunting
> #51 in Kindle Store > Kindle eBooks > Nonfiction > Self-Help > Creativity

You can click on the different categories, such as Job Hunting or Creativity in this case. What you want to look for are categories where you have a chance to be #1.

To figure this out, look for categories relevant to your book where the #1 spot is held by someone with a

Paid Sales Rank of #20,000 or higher. A #20,000 rank means the book is selling around 4-6 copies per day.

The way you check this is to click on a category, click on the #1 book, and check their sales rank. Now, you may not find a category with these numbers. I rarely do. If you do, great. If you don't, pick the best category you can find. Don't worry too much about it.

3. Description

Your cover and title pull people in, but your description tells the reader if your book is right for them.

Once again, if you're starting out, don't expect to come up with an amazing description, unless you're willing to put in the work and study good book descriptions, or good copywriting. You can tweak your description whenever you want, so you can't make any huge mistakes.

The best way to write a description is to find books that have descriptions that resonate with you. Then use the description as a template. In other words, notice what about the description speaks to you and use the same elements in your book description.

For example, the description for my book, *Find Your Passion*, has the following structure:

Headline
Attention-grabbing introduction
What you'll learn
What you'll experience
Bullet points
Call to action (grab the book)

Don't try to get your description perfect. Look at a description you like, throw in your keywords a few times, and put yourself in the shoes of your ideal reader. Be honest and share who your book is for.

4. Author Central

Once your book is published, go to http://authorcentral.amazon.com/, create an account, and claim your book.

It will make your name clickable in each book you claim. This allows you to put in an author bio, link to your site, and it gives readers an overview of all of your (claimed) books.

You can see my bio here:
http://www.wakeupcloud.com/books

Don't be afraid to share your story in your bio. Let people connect with you. That's what this is all about.

Now let's look at the other part of selling, which is building your platform. Optimizing your Amazon listing is all well and good, but it doesn't matter if you don't have people coming in contact with your book.

3 Tips for Building Your Platform

You may have heard these tips over and over again, but have you applied them? It's easy to dismiss these as "nothing new," but the fact remains that they work. How do I know? Because I've used them since 2009.

1. Start a Blog

This isn't just about blogging. This is about building a platform—a community where your readers can gather and learn more about you.

The bigger your platform, the easier it will be for you to launch books. If you don't know how to start a blog, I've put together a comprehensive free guide over at my blog: http://www.wakeupcloud.com/how-to-start-a-blog/

A blog doesn't have to take all of your time. You can adapt a blog to fit your needs. But above all else, you need to go out there and let the world know that you exist and that you have a story to tell.

2. Promote

I've built my blog from 0 to 10,000+ subscribers almost solely through guest blogging, which means writing articles for other websites and blogs.

If you want a free guide on how to guest blog, and how I do it, go here: http://www.wakeupcloud.com/guest-blogging-guide/

You have to find the right promotional strategy for you. It doesn't matter where you start, as long as you start and observe the results you get.

You could comment on blogs where your ideal reader is likely to be.

You could hang out in forums.

You could do interviews.

You could create something that people want to share with others.

There are whole books written about building a platform, but to me it comes down to trying a lot of things until you find what works. Start with what you deem doable, and see what happens.

3. Build an Email List

Last, but not least, build an email list. This is critical. It is through my email list that I've been able to launch my books, and to make a living online.

An email list is an online newsletter. People sign up, and you can stay in touch with them over a period of time. You can build a relationship with them.

How do you build an email list? You have something to offer. For example, on my blog, I give away a free report when you sign up to my email list. After you've signed up, I send you new articles, tips, free books, and offers from time to time.

If you need a good email marketing service, I use Aweber.com.

The biggest mistake you can make is to not build an email list. You can come up with reasons for why you shouldn't, but sooner or later, you will realize that this is a mistake.

Example

When I launch a new book, I announce it to my email list. That's the extent of my marketing strategy. I could do better, and I probably will in the future, but for now, I'm happy with this.

In other words, my work has gone in before I even started writing books. I've built an audience on my blog of thousands of readers that want to hear from me.

When I launch a new book, people are interested, because I listen to my audience, and I write on topics that help them move toward what they want.

Sometimes I launch my books for free. Sometimes I give my readers a discount for a few days. But the bottom line is that I've built a platform from which I can launch books, programs, and anything that helps my readers.

It's never too late to start, but you have to be willing to see through your fears and excuses.

Books I Recommend

If you want to learn more about promotion and selling, I have three recommendations for you:

> 1. *61 Ways to Sell More Nonfiction Kindle Books* by Steve Scott
> 2. *Your First 1000 Copies: The Step-by-Step Guide to Marketing Your Book* by Tim Grohl
> 3. *Write. Publish. Repeat. (The No-Luck-Required Guide to Self-Publishing Success)* by Sean Platt and Johnny B Truant

Before you read any of these, remember to get your book out there. Don't get caught up in the details. Not yet. First write, then tweak.

Action Steps

Let's look at the action steps:

> **1. Optimize Listing.** Find the right keywords for your book. If you've already written your book,

don't worry about it. You can do this for your next book. Find the right categories. Write a good description, and create an account on Amazon author central.

2. Platform. Build an audience that is interested in what you have to offer. You may not know how to do this, or where to even start. Don't worry, you will figure it out as you go. I wasn't crystal clear when I started. Most people aren't. What matters is action.

3. Common Sense. Don't rely on anyone's advice. There are no rules. There are guidelines, yes, but in the end, you have to rely on your common sense. Listen to what feels right for you. You will want to get things perfect, but remember, this is about progress, not perfection. The only way to learn is to write, and write some more.

Yes, this can seem like a lot of stuff, but writing isn't a way to get rich quick. This is about a life-long journey. There's no rush anywhere. Focus on enjoying the writing, and let the results take care of themselves. Your job is to write, the rest is up to life.

Summary

We've gone through a lot, and your brain may be overflowing, so here's a quick summary of what you've learned.

1. The Intersection

We started by covering the importance of finding the intersection between what you want to write, and what people want to read. You discover what people want to read by looking at what's already out there, such as books on Amazon.

2. The Title

Then we dipped our toes in coming up with a title, which came down to looking at titles you like, making a promise, and brainstorming.

3. Ideal Reader

You also learned about writing for an ideal reader, which you can find by focusing on a client, a friend, or a past version of you.

4. Creative Brainstorm

The creative brainstorm was about priming your subconscious mind. Your action steps were to freewrite and organize your material into a messy outline for your book. Once you've pushed yourself to the edge, you let go, and let your subconscious do the work.

5. Book Blueprint

Next, you wrote down an outline for the chapters of your book. You looked at your creative brainstorm and threw something together. No perfection needed, just progress.

6. Chapter Blueprint

Then you did the same thing for each of your chapters. You took one chapter, and you outlined it with the same process as you did with the book blueprint.

7. Chapter Notes

Finally, you wrote notes under each subheading in each chapter. These notes are like stepping stones. They keep you on track as you write your first horrible draft.

8. Horrible First Draft

With your blueprints and notes in place, it's time for your first draft, your first horrible draft. Pick the easiest chapter, and start freewriting. Don't stop to edit. Don't censor. Dump whatever is on your mind on paper. If you get stuck, turn your subheadings into questions.

9. Germination

When your first draft is done, let your book germinate for a week or two. During this time, capture any inspirational bursts, and put them in the relevant chapter.

10. Second Draft

After a few weeks, write your second draft. The second draft for me is all about making my book readable. I go through the material from my freewriting sessions, and I simplify, reword, and tweak.

11. "Final" Draft

After letting my second draft sit for a while (the amount of time is up to you, always), I go through my book a third time. The third draft is often about changing how I word things, and removing a few thousand words from my book, to make it easier to read.

12. Getting Feedback

Once the third revision is done, I send out my book to interested readers. I want to get honest, constructive feedback that helps me improve my book and see what I've missed.

13. Working With an Editor

After relevant feedback has been implemented, I send my book to my editor, who spots any remaining typos or errors.

14. Designing Your Book

Then I work with a designer to create my cover. I often start working with my designer while I'm writing my book, just to make sure that my cover is done when my book is done.

15. Formatting

Formatting is a piece of cake with Scrivener (my software of choice). I write my book, and all I have to do is export it to Kindle format (or whatever format I need).

16. Pricing

Then we covered pricing, where I basically said that if your goal is to sell as many books as possible, choose a lower price (below \$2.99), and if you want to make money while selling more books to choose a middle price (around \$2.99). This applies to Amazon.

For PDF books—and books you sell via your website—your price will depend on what you offer. If it's just a book, a lower price is often wise. If you sell a package of text, audio, video, workbooks, and so on, you can charge more, because there's more value.

17. Selling

Finally, we covered selling, where I share some simple tips for publishing on Amazon. I also told you about building your own platform. When you have an audience of people that want to hear from you, you can do so much, so don't put if off.

That's it for the summary. Let's move on to the conclusion and wrap things up.

Conclusion

Let me be completely honest: I'm not a world-class writer. I have fears. I sometimes want to crawl under my bed covers and hide. But I write because I can't not write. I love writing.

You've read this book because deep down you want to write, too. You have fears. We all do, but the key is to start. It doesn't matter if you've never written a single word.

You don't need permission from anyone to write. You just have to start. You will meet dragons on your journey, and that's how it should be.

Write because you feel inspired to write. No other reason is necessary. And above all, keep writing, no matter what anyone says or thinks, and no matter what ideas fear tries to sell you.

Always keep writing.

And always follow your inspiration, because it is what guides you through this thing we call life.

Your Bonus

In the beginning of this book, I promised you a free gift.

This free gift is a workbook with the relevant action steps and questions from each chapter put together in a PDF file, which allows you to print it out for easy referencing.

You don't have to sign up for anything. Just grab the workbook on the link below:

http://www.wakeupcloud.com/goodies/WriteEbooksWorkbook.pdf

Resources

Below are most of the recommendations I've made in this book.

Software

Use a search engine to find the software below. The links change from time to time, so a quick search is an easy way to find them.

Microsoft Word
Scrivener
FreeMind (mind-mapping software)

Books

Accidental Genius by Mark Levy
Psycho-Cybernetics by Maxwell Maltz
61 Ways to Sell More Nonfiction Kindle Books by Steve Scott
Your First 1000 Copies: The Step-by-Step Guide to Marketing Your Book by Tim Grohl
Write. Publish. Repeat. (The No-Luck-Required Guide to Self-Publishing Success) by Sean Platt and Johnny B Truant

Blog Posts

How to Start a Blog –
http://www.wakeupcloud.com/how-to-start-a-blog/
Guest Blogging Guide –
http://www.wakeupcloud.com/guest-blogging-guide/

Podcast Episodes

How to Create Life-Changing Online Courses –
http://www.wakeupcloud.com/8/
How to Make a Living Writing Books –
http://www.wakeupcloud.com/15/
Increase Your Writing Speed by 300% –
http://www.wakeupcloud.com/11/

Services / Websites

Aweber (Email Marketing) - http://www.aweber.com/
Upwork – http://www.upwork.com
Fiverr - http://www.fiverr.com/
Charfish Design - http://www.charfishdesign.com/
Anna (Editor) - http://www.annaparadox.com/

Connect

If you'd like to learn more about me, head on over to my blog at http://www.wakeupcloud.com/ and specifically my About page at http://www.wakeupcloud.com/about/

I have a free newsletter where I send out exclusive tips on a regular basis on how to do work you love. So if you're interested in learning more, I invite you to visit my website.

And as I mentioned earlier, if you have any questions, comments, or just want to say hi, feel free to email me at henri@wakeupcloud.com.

Books

If you liked this book, you may be interested in my other books. You'll find them below.

My books are available in all Amazon stores, so if you're outside the U.S, all you have to do is search for these books, or my name (Henri Junttila), and you'll find them. If you don't, email me at henri@wakeupcloud.com, and I'll help you out.

Below is a list of some of my other books that might interest you:

Find Your Passion:
25 Questions You Must Ask Yourself

Follow Your Heart:
21 Days to a Happier, More Fulfilling Life

Write Blog Posts Readers Love:
A Step-By-Step Guide

All of these books are available on Amazon. You can find them, along with an updated list of my books, at http://www.wakeupcloud.com/books

96963215R00070

Made in the USA
Lexington, KY
25 August 2018